Lion Pride

Julie Murray

Abdo Kids Junior
is an Imprint of Abdo Kids
abdopublishing.com

Abdo
ANIMAL GROUPS
Kids

abdopublishing.com

Published by Abdo Kids, a division of ABDO, P.O. Box 398166, Minneapolis, Minnesota 55439. Copyright © 2019 by Abdo Consulting Group, Inc. International copyrights reserved in all countries. No part of this book may be reproduced in any form without written permission from the publisher. Abdo Kids Junior™ is a trademark and logo of Abdo Kids.

Printed in the United States of America, North Mankato, Minnesota.

052018

092018

Photo Credits: iStock, Shutterstock

Production Contributors: Teddy Borth, Jennie Forsberg, Grace Hansen

Design Contributors: Christina Doffing, Candice Keimig, Dorothy Toth

Library of Congress Control Number: 2017960608

Publisher's Cataloging-in-Publication Data

Names: Murray, Julie, author.

Title: Lion pride / by Julie Murray.

Description: Minneapolis, Minnesota : Abdo Kids, 2019. | Series: Animal groups | Includes glossary, index and online resources (page 24).

Identifiers: ISBN 9781532107818 (lib.bdg.) | ISBN 9781532108792 (ebook) | ISBN 9781532109287 (Read-to-me ebook)

Subjects: LCSH: Lion--Behavior--Juvenile literature. | Animal behavior--Juvenile literature. | Social behavior in animals--Juvenile literature. | Animal species--Juvenile literature.

Classification: DDC 599.757--dc23

Table of Contents

Lion Pride 4

Being in a Pride 22

Glossary. 23

Index 24

Abdo Kids Code. 24

Lion Pride

Lions are big cats. Most lions live in Africa.

Lions live in a group. It is called a pride.

A pride has 10 to 40 lions.

They live in one area. They hunt, play, and sleep there.

There are 1 to 3 males. They **protect** the pride. They roar to keep others away.

Many females are in the group.

They raise the cubs.

Females hunt for food.

They work together.

The pride licks one another.

They show their love.

19

They also **nuzzle**. They are saying hello.

Being in a Pride

10 to 40 in a pride

hunt together

live in an area (territory)

nuzzle each other

Glossary

nuzzle
to touch, push, or rub the nose against.

protect
to keep safe from harm.

Index

Africa 4

clean 18

communication 20

cubs 14

females 14, 16

food 16

hunt 10, 16

males 12

members 8, 12, 14, 16

nuzzle 20

protect 12

territory 10

Visit **abdokids.com** and use this code to access crafts, games, videos, and more!

Abdo Kids Code:
ALK7818